MW01140489

THROUGH THE BIBLE IN 40 RIDDLES

RICK BASSETT

ILLUSTRATED BY
MARIA CHRISTINA NEL LOPEZ

Published in Dallas, Texas by Honeydrop Kids Club
www.honeydropkids.com
Illustrated by: Maria Christina Nel Lopez
ISBN# 978-1088007877

DEDICATION

I'd like to dedicate this book to my grandchildren who inspired it --
Aubrial, Isaiah, Hansen, Titus, Theo, Emmaus, Miriam, Levi and Nori.
You got my creative juices flowing, helping me to look at the greatest
story ever told through the eyes of a child once again!

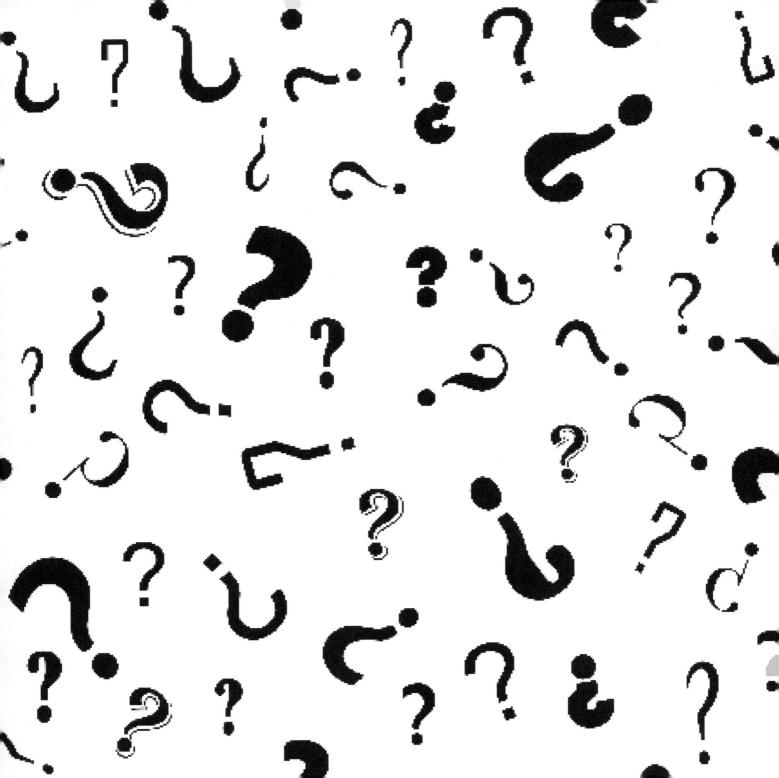

A NOTE TO PARENTS & TEACHERS:

Several years ago, I wanted to find a way to maintain a better connection with my grandchildren. They live in Michigan, and I live in California, so I had the idea of crafting Bible riddles where they would read the riddle, then follow the clue that would lead them to the answer in the Bible. When they answered correctly, I would reward them with money ($1) and then send them another riddle.

Well, that idea blossomed into Through the Bible in 40 Riddles, which captures the overall story in scripture from the Garden of Eden to the Garden in Paradise. The goal of the 40 Riddles is to help children have fun while reading the Bible, to help them begin to see the storyline that runs throughout, to teach them how to read the Bible with some understanding, and to help kids get some hands-on experience in using the Bible.

As their parent or teacher, your role is to help them find the answer to the clues in the Your Mission section and then, find a way to reward them with candy, money, etc. so that God's Word might taste "sweeter than honey" (Psalm 19:10). Personally, I know the power of being drawn into the Bible and being changed through it. I got "hooked" at age of 16 and it changed my life. I hope the children in your life experience its life-giving impact as well.

Rick Bassett

P.S. In the back this book, there's an answer key and glossary for you to use as a quick reference guide!

THIS BOOK IS A GIFT TO:

_____

FROM:

_____

DATE:

_____

DEAR READER,

Most stories make you use your imagination when you read them. Well, the story in the Bible does that and so much more. It invites you to become part of the story yourself! Do you know what that is? Begin the journey of Through the Bible in 40 Riddles and begin to find out!

Here's how this works:

- Read the riddle. (Read them in order. Try not to skip ahead.)
- Your mission is to take the clues and go find the answers in your Bible.
- Once you find them, write them in the space below.
- If you get stuck on some of the words, or want to check your answers, there's a glossary and answer key in the back of the book.

I hope you enjoy!

Rick Bassett

Author

CREATION

BIBLE RIDDLE #1 :

Now, God made sky, water, land, and seas,
corn, *alfalfa*, and honeybees,
Sun and moon and stars above --
and big gray elephants that would give a shove.
The question remains: How did He set it all in motion?
Was it with a wand, fairy dust, or magic potion?
If you'll look closely you'll see just how
God made the dog, the cat, and the dairy cow.

YOUR MISSION

Describe how God made all of these things.

_____

_____

_____

_____

_____

_____

_____

_____

_____

_____

_____

CLUES:

Read Genesis 1:3, 6, 9, 11, 14, 20, 24, 26

BIBLE RIDDLE #2:

When God was nearly done making all creation,
He made something else that caused a celebration.
For birds and bees were not at the top.
No, He made something else that was the
"cream of the crop".
Because if everything He made was kind of the same,
that would make this world just all too tame.
So God made a creature in His likeness,
which the animals saw and thought, "Look, there's our *Highness!*"

Nothing could be clearer.
Just look in the mirror.

YOUR MISSION

Who was the most special creature that God made?

CLUES:

Read Genesis 1:26-28

BIBLE RIDDLE #3

Now when God finished making man,
He said, "He can't just stand there...
He needs work for his hands."
So, God gave man something to do,
something important for the whole human crew.
And unlike the other creatures he made,
God gave him work for which his heart would *crave*.
One job was family. The other with the creatures.
Can you tell me the two jobs that man was to feature?

YOUR MISSION

What two jobs did God give to people?

CLUES:

Read Genesis 1:28

BIBLE RIDDLE #4:

When, after 6 days, God had made everything,
did He take time to wipe his brow or sing?
After all, it was a lot to make;
A lot more than baking a chocolate cake!
Did He stand back with a *furrowed* brow
and say, "It's ok…it'll do for now"?
Or did a happy smile cross His face
As he looked at all he made out of empty space?
Now, look real close at what God thought of his labor,

'cause it'll affect what you think of yourself and your neighbor.

YOUR MISSION:

What did God think of all the He had made?

_____

_____

_____

_____

_____

_____

_____

_____

_____

_____

_____

CLUES:

Read Genesis 1:31

BIBLE RIDDLE #5

God made a lot of things that were pretty and pure,
and what He made was *good* for sure.
But did He have to work each and every day?
Or was there any time for rest and play?
Because if all God did was Creation chores,
when was there time to eat chocolate S'mores?
So tell me what God did on the 7th day,

after 6 days of making bunnies, berries, and hay?

YOUR MISSION

What did God do on the 7th day?

_____

_____

_____

_____

_____

_____

_____

_____

_____

_____

CLUES:

Read Genesis 2:2-3

BIBLE RIDDLE #6

At first Adam's life seemed like it was a breeze,
just take care of animals and start a family.
But God wanted to know what Adam most loved.
Would it be his own desires or God up above?
So with a tree, God gave Adam a choice,
would Adam follow God or someone else's voice?
So in the Garden God placed a tree of *temptation*.

Something that could cause Adam great *devastation*.

YOUR MISSION

1. What was the name of the tree of temptation?

2. What would happen if Adam ate from that tree?

CLUES:

Read Genesis 2:17

BIBLE RIDDLE #7

A crafty serpent crawled up to Eve and whispered in her ear,
"The forbidden tree's not so bad, just take a bite, my dear!
Because when it's fruit slides down your thirsty throat,
You'll be smart like God, and not stupid like a goat."
Well, Eve was enchanted by the Serpent's offer,
and enticed by the possibility of being a whole lot smarter
So, she picked the fruit and took a bite, just as the Serpent said,
and gave some to her husband, who -- now disobeying God -- wasn't using his head
Now, once they both had eaten what God had said they shouldn't,
their eyes saw something scary that God really wished they wouldn't
and their life in paradise was ruined!

YOUR MISSION

1. What did they see that scared them?
2. What did they do to deal with their problem?
3. What did they do when they heard the Lord God walking among the trees in the Garden?

CLUES:

For questions 1 & 2, read Genesis 3:7

For question 3, read Genesis 3:8

THE CURSE

BIBLE RIDDLE #8

Eating the forbidden fruit caused the whole world to spoil.
One had to crawl, one cried, and the third for food would toil.
We still struggle with the first couple's *rebellion* --
Whether in childbirth, work, or all things *reptilian*.
So remember where all the sad things started,
so that you can find out how not to be broken-hearted.
And when you think about the clues this story taught,
the key for us is to love the Lord with all we've got.

YOUR MISSION

1. What happened to the serpent that tricked Adam and Eve?
2. What happened to the woman because of her disobedience?

3. What happened to Adam because of his disobedience?

_____

_____

_____

_____

_____

_____

_____

_____

_____

_____

_____

_____

CLUES:
For Question 1: Read Genesis 3:14-15
For Question 2: Read Genesis 3:16
For Question 3: Read Genesis 3:17-19

BIBLE RIDDLE #9

You have to go now. No more living in Eden's shade,
Instead you must work the ground from which you were made.
But before you go, don't forget these,
they work a lot better as clothes

than leaves from the trees.

YOUR MISSION
What did God clothe Adam and Eve with

that worked better than leaves?

CLUES:
Compare Genesis 3:21 to Genesis 3:7

22

FAMILY

BIBLE RIDDLE #10

Adam and Eve were very sad,
for the things they'd done that were so very bad.
Even their boys got into fighting,
instead of as brothers and family *uniting*.
So, what could help them with all of their tears,
and chase away their many fears?
Well, Adam and Eve had another son,
who somehow figured out what could be done.
Yes, this boy started something new,
that you and I and everyone can do.
And if you'll read closely you'll see what's there,

it rhymes with a very pleasant word called "care".

YOUR MISSION

What did men start doing in the days of Seth and Enosh,
Adam and Eve's son and grandson?

_____

_____

_____

_____

_____

_____

_____

_____

_____

_____

CLUES:

Read Genesis 4:25-26

BIBLE RIDDLE #11

Now it's time for some "Adam's Family" history,
so that those old days aren't just one big mystery.
You see, the first sons of Adam lived on and on,
'til they bounced on their knees their great, great grandsons.
Two of them especially stand out in the crowd,
one lived really long and the other left in a cloud.

YOUR MISSION

1. Name the man who lived longer than anyone else,
and how long he lived.
2. Name the man who didn't die but just disappeared,
and explain why he was special.

CLUES:

1. Read Genesis 5:26-27
2. Read Genesis 5:21-24

28

THE FLOOD

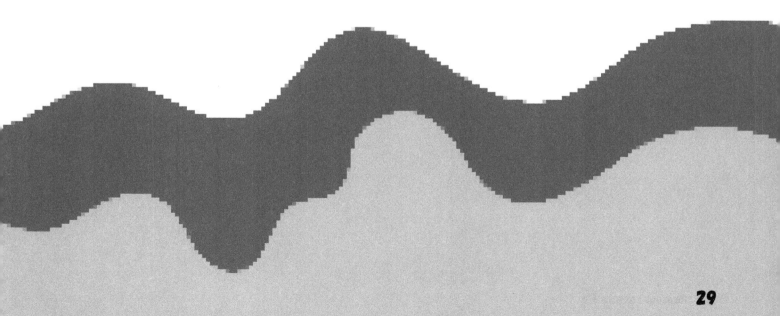

BIBLE RIDDLE #12

While Methuselah lived really, really long,
and Enoch's time with God was really strong,
most of the people were so very bad,
that it made God's heart really sad.
So God came up with a brand new plan,
to remove these wicked people from the land.
But one man's goodness just stood out,
too much for God to wipe everyone out.
So God told this man to build something HUGE
that could handle an unheard of watery *deluge*.
And to take some folks and critters on board,
so that they wouldn't drown in the rain that poured.
So while all of the wicked people died,
this one, good man and his "friends" survived.

YOUR MISSION

1. Who was this good man God used to save people?
2. What was the "Ark"?
3. Who rode on the "Ark"?

4. Why did Noah take animals on the Ark?

(blank lined writing area)

CLUES:

1. Read Genesis 6:8,9,13

2. Read Genesis 6:14-18 and Genesis 7:11-13

3. Read Genesis 7:1-3

4. Read Genesis 7:3

THE PATRIARCHS

BIBLE RIDDLE #13

Well, Noah, the good man, finally died.
After his boat and clothes and dirt all dried.
Then Noah's sons all had sons and daughters,
since they alone survived the flood waters.
But the problems of man still brought them shame,
since their sinful hearts remained the same.
So, God had another plan up his sleeve,
He thought, "I'll find a man who's willing to leave.
And when he says "goodbye" to his dad,
he's gonna look back on that day and be glad.
Because I, God, will make his family great,
so great that no sacrifice could possibly taint.
Yes, I will bless those who bless you,
and curse those who curse you.
And because of you, for every nation,
there'll be a reason for global celebration.
And so, this man, at 75, departed.
(Pretty old for someone just getting started.)
But he, and we, should be really glad,

because he showed us how to relate to our Heavenly Dad.

YOUR MISSION

What is the name of the man who left his dad
at God's command,
and then was blessed?

CLUES:

Read Genesis 12:1-4

BIBLE RIDDLE #14

So, Abraham believed God which made everything right.
Now he and God could be really, really tight.
Well, Abraham's story was just getting started,
as he packed his wife and nephew
and from Haran departed.
25 years later he had Isaac, a miracle boy,
giving Abraham and his wife, Sarah, hilarious joy!
Then Isaac himself would grow up to be a dad,
so happy to be the father of twins...*egad*!
The twins would grow up and get into a *tussle*,
but this fight wasn't won by the brother with the most muscle.
The older twin, Esau, sold his birthright...really dumb.
And now through the younger son, Jacob, the promise would come.
Jacob would marry and have 12 boys,
one especially, Joseph, gave him the most joy.
When Joseph was given a beautiful coat by his dad,
that made the other brothers really mad!
One day, while the other brothers were out grazing the sheep,
they looked into the distance and saw him coming
and thought, "let's seize the little creep!"
They grabbed him, took his coat, and put him in a hole,
then later by his brothers, as a slave, he was sold.

Yes, Joseph wound up where he didn't want to be,
but God had a great plan for the whole family.

YOUR MISSION

1. How much was Joseph sold for?
2. Where was he taken as a slave?
3. Who became his master?

CLUES:

1. Read Genesis 37:28
2. Read Genesis 37:28,36
3. Read Genesis 37:36

BIBLE RIDDLE #15

In Egypt, Joseph started off kind of bad,
but after a while he made his new master glad.
Because God gave Joseph such great success,
his master said, "To all my house you now have access."
But one day Joseph caught a married woman's eye,
who said, "You've got to be my boyfriend or I'll just die!"
But Joseph knew that wouldn't be right,
so he left his coat and got out of her sight.
When the woman lied to her husband about the details,
her husband had Joseph thrown into a stinky jail.
But even there, when things turned out worse than expected,
Joseph, the slave-turned-prisoner, became highly respected.
And when Joseph, while in prison, used a special gift,
That God-given talent gave him a mighty lift.
Because he became the second most powerful man,
in all of that mighty and *influential* land.

YOUR MISSION

1. Who was Joseph's master?
2. Who wanted Joseph to be her lover?
3. What did Joseph do that turned him into a powerful leader of Egypt?

CLUES:

1. Read Genesis 39:1
2. Read Genesis 39:6-12
3. Read Genesis 41:15-16,
25-27, 33-40

BIBLE RIDDLE #16

Joseph, the leader, saved extra grain for a "rainy day"
So, all the people could eat when the grain went away.
And so, when his family back home ran out of food,
the famine brought them to his Egyptian neighborhood.
Now when the brothers met him
as the man in charge of the food they craved,
they didn't recognize him as the one they had enslaved.
So, Joseph tested them to see if they were sad,
about the things they'd done to him that were oh so bad.
And when he found out that they had changed for the better,
he cried out loud and said, "Hey! It's me, your brother!"
When the brothers saw this ruler was their brother in the flesh,
they all gave each other a big group hug and kiss.
And Joseph's dad, Jacob, was beyond belief thrilled,
that his dearly beloved son hadn't actually been killed.
So Joseph's family moved south to this Egyptian land,
where a new chapter was written in God's rescue plan.

YOUR MISSION

1. Which brother offered to become a slave in Egypt to protect his little brother and dad?
2. According to Joseph, what was God intending to do when Joseph was sold into slavery by his brothers?

CLUES:

1. Read Genesis 44:18-34 (key verses are 18,33,34)
2. Read Genesis 45:5; 50:20

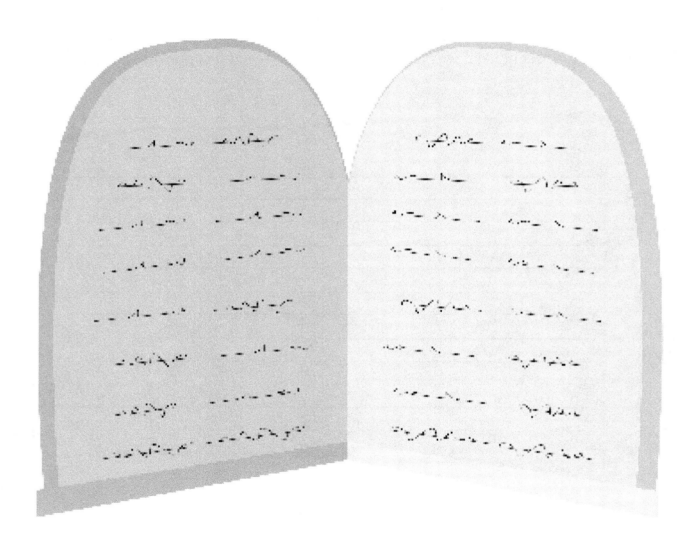

42

BIBLE RIDDLE #17

Joseph and his brothers eventually passed away,
and another Pharaoh came who didn't remember their names.
Now, because Joseph's family really increased and grew,
this new Pharaoh made them do the only thing he knew to do.
He made the Hebrews slaves who would experience blood, sweat, and tears.
That lasted a miserable 400 years!
Finally God heard their cries and misery,
and sent them a *deliverer* from the baby nursery.
And while his beginning seemed pretty innocent,
God would use this boy to do something magnificent.

YOUR MISSION

1. What did Pharaoh do to the Hebrew baby boys?
2. Where was one Hebrew baby hidden, who would later become Israel's deliverer?
3. What was the name of the baby boy who would become Israel's deliverer?

CLUES:

1. Read Exodus 1:22
2. Read Exodus 2:1-3
3. Read Exodus 2:10

BIBLE RIDDLE #18

After baby Moses had grown into a man,
he killed an Egyptian and buried him in the sand.
Not wanting to get caught, he went on the run,
and came to live in Midian under the hot, hot sun.
One day, while he was leading some sheep to food.
He looked over and saw a burning bush that wasn't consumed.
So, he stepped aside to take a look, to see what he could see,
when the Lord said from within the bush, "I've seen Israel's misery.
And now, Moses, I'm calling you to do something brave - -
go and lead my people, out of the land where they're slaves.
That's right, stop tending sheep to make all of your money,
go to Egypt and lead my people to the land of milk and honey!"

YOUR MISSION

1. Why did God tell Moses to take off his sandals at the burning bush?
2. What reason for confidence did God give Moses that he could lead the Israelites out of Egypt?
3. What name was Moses supposed to give the Israelites when they asked him, "Who sent you?"

CLUES:

1. Read Exodus 3:5
2. Read Exodus 3:11-12
3. Read Exodus 3:13-14

BIBLE RIDDLE #19

Moses went to Egypt to talk to Pharaoh,
about God's saving command to "Let my people go!"
But every time Moses made his demand,
Pharaoh said, "No!" with his scepter thrust in the sand. Even
when God sent plagues with great precision,
Pharaoh wouldn't budge from his hard-hearted decision.
From water too bloody for a cool, refreshing drink,
to frogs and gnats and flies that clogged up the sink.
From dead animals and boils that really, really hurt,
to hailstones and locusts that ate everything but dirt.
And when three days of darkness didn't cut Israel any slack,
God sent a 10th plague that would "break the camel's back."

YOUR MISSION

1. What was the 10th plague God sent that made Pharaoh free the Hebrew slaves?
2. What is the name of the ceremony that remembers the 10th plague?

CLUES:

1. Read Exodus 11:1, 5 & Exodus 23:29-30
2. Read Exodus 12:25-27 (key verse is 27)

BIBLE RIDDLE #20
The Exodus - 13-15

When Israel left their 400 years of misery,
they had second thoughts about their God-given destiny.
For as they looked behind them, they saw hot -on -their- heels,
600 chariots made of hardened steel.
They said, "It'd be better to be an Egyptian slave,
then to end up six-feet under in a dry, desert grave."
But Moses said, "Don't be afraid of their chariots,
because the whole world will see that for you, God fought."
Just then the angel and pillar of cloud got stationed between,
so that by the Egyptians Israel couldn't be seen.
And as Moses *obediently* stretched out this hand,
the Lord drove the sea back, turning it into dry land.
So, the Israelites, with walls of water on each side,
walked through the ocean and not one person died.
But the Egyptians thought, "Now's the perfect time to attack!"
And chased them, only in horror to watch the water flow back.
Yes, not one Egyptian warrior survived the collapsed walls of water,
leaving behind *grieving widows*, sons, and daughters.
It was one of Israel's all-time greatest victories,
a story that would be written in world history.

YOUR MISSION

When the Israelites saw the power of God at the crossing of the Red Sea, how did it affect their relationship with God and with Moses?

_____

_____

_____

_____

_____

_____

_____

_____

_____

_____

_____

CLUES:

Read Exodus 14:31

BIBLE RIDDLE #21

When Israel left Egypt they were more than a million people,
which is more than you could fit in a church with a steeple.
So they started their journey back to the Promised Land,
guided by Moses' voice and God's strong hand.
But the people kept showing their unbelief,
when they focused all their attention on bodily relief.
Yes, food and water and safety are essential,
but they shouldn't it make you doubt God's *sterling credentials.*
For when all the people got thirsty for a drink,
God used a stick and rock for water and not the kitchen sink!
And when there wasn't any tasty food at their table,
God again showed the nation he was more than able.
So, if you feel thirst and hunger clawing at your insides,
remember that God Almighty is the God who provides!

YOUR MISSION

1. What was the name of the first place God miraculously provided water for Israel?
2. What was the name of the two foods God provided for Israel?

CLUES:

1. Read Exodus 15:22-25
2. Read Exodus 16:11-15, 31

EXTRA CREDIT: WHAT IS THE MEANING OF THE NAME OF THE BREAD? (CLUE: READ EXODUS 16:31 PLUS THE FOOTNOTE)

BIBLE RIDDLE #22

Israel made it through those first free weeks.
'Cause God provided all their needs in food and drink.
So they set up camp at the base of Sinai Mountain,
where God's Word came to Moses like a fresh spring fountain.
The Lord said, "You're going to be my treasured possession,
if you'll make my holy ways your daily obsession."
"Yes, out of all the peoples you will be a holy nation,
just keep my 10 commands," was the invitation.
So Moses hiked down with God's Word carved on a rock
but God's voice they didn't hear cause it would send em' into shock!
Now the question remains, "Would God's presence they fear,
or would they forget his ways and their own life *steer*?"

YOUR MISSION

1. What was God's 1st command to the Israelites?
2. What was his 5th command?
3. What was his 8th command?

CLUES:

1. Read Exodus 20:3
2. Read Exodus 20:12
3. Read Exodus 20:15

56

JOSHUA

BIBLE RIDDLE #23

After Moses climbed a mountain and all heard that he was dead,
God said to Joshua, "You'll lead my people instead."
"Like I said, I'll give you land where ever you place your feet,
and no matter how tough the people are, they're enemies that I'll beat.
"You're gonna take a lot of space so be sure that you are strong,
and when it is all done, to you, Canaan will belong.
"I know that it's the kind of job that makes hearts fear,
but don't give into fear at all cause I, your God, am near."
Now Joshua's first test was the kind that makes spines shiver.
He had to lead a million people across a flooded river!
But when the priests walked into it with the Ark held on their shoulders,
the river dried and 12 men took 12 wet now dry rock boulders!

YOUR MISSION

1. Who would be with Joshua to help him be courageous and not afraid?
2. What was the name of the flooded river they had to cross?
3. What happened to the river when the priests stepped in the water?

CLUES:

1. Read Joshua 1:9
2. Read Joshua 1:2

BIBLE RIDDLE #24

Crossin' the Jordan was only the beginning,
kind of like playin' baseball in the very first inning.
So they sent two spies to spy out the land,
where they met a woman in Jericho named "Rahab".
She told em', "We're too scared to stand up to y'all!"
That's when the spies knew that Jericho's walls would fall.
God told em', "March the 7th day 'round the wall 7 times,
then when you're done have the people give a real loud cry!"
When they gave the "shout!" the walls did collapse and crumble,
leaving its scared people to moan and mumble.
Well they kept up their mission to take all Canaan,
beating kings like Dor, Hazor, Hormah, Gezer and Hebron.
Then the time came for God to divide up the land,
givin' each group the promised dirt to Israel's 12 clans.
And when old Joshua saw his death in sight,
he had a final thing to say before he "turned out the lights".
"As you've watched all God's done to give you rewards,
it's time you gave yourselves to Him and serve the Lord!"

YOUR MISSION
Who did the people agree to serve after Joshua's challenge to them?

_____
_____
_____
_____
_____
_____
_____
_____
_____
_____
_____

CLUES:
Read Joshua 24:19-22

THE JUDGES

BIBLE RIDDLE #25

Joshua died at one-hundred and ten,
which is when the Israelites fell deep into sin.
You see the good God did, they just forgot,
and then their life in Canaan would start to rot.
The recipe for misery was, "serve the *Baals*",
and that's when everything in their lives would fail.
But because God wouldn't keep holdin' a grudge,
He decided to relieve em' and so sent em' a judge.
Like Deborah who wasn't in an all-girl band,
God used her smarts to help kill Sisera, a bad army man.
There was Gideon, who with 300 trumpets and lights,
smashed a hoard of eastern peoples called 'Midianites'.
And when all the judges were almost done,
God sent a really strong one named "Samson".
Now the secret to his strength was his uncut hair,
which gave him strength to kill a lion coming out of his *lair*.
At his end, Samson killed 3000 Philistines,
when he pushed with all his might on their temple's main beams.
After that, for a while, Israel had no leader,
who could keep the nation from the brink instead of *teeter*.
So now, for Israel, it remained to be seen,
if they would get another leader to be their king.

YOUR MISSION

What did the people do because they didn't have a king?

CLUES:

Read Judges 21:25

SAMUEL, KING SAUL, & KING DAVID

BIBLE RIDDLE #26

A sad woman named Hannah really wanted a son,
a boy she'd give to God who would serve him a ton.
Well Hannah's son, Samuel, learned to hear God's voice,
Which helped him as he grew to make the very best choice.
One day God told Samuel, "Give Israel what they asked for, give them a king…
But warn them that he'll be so *oppressing*."
Then Samuel crossed paths with a man named Saul,
who couldn't hide in a crowd 'cause he was so tall.
Samuel crowned Saul as Israel's very first king.
The kind of king who'd do a lot of stumbling.
Saul started strong in his royal career,
but later fell flat 'cause God's Word he didn't fear.
So, Samuel went looking for another king.
A king for whom God would mean everything.
Samuel found his man in a shepherd boy,
A young man named David, Saul would try to destroy.
And as this drama finally came to an end,
Saul died in war while David's *reign* would begin.

YOUR MISSION

What was one way king Saul disobeyed the Lord?

_____

_____

_____

_____

_____

_____

_____

_____

_____

_____

_____

CLUES:

Read 1 Samuel 15:17-19

BIBLE RIDDLE #27

When David was a boy he watched his daddy's flocks,
writin' songs called "Psalms" while sittin' on rocks.
Then Samuel came to town to David's dad, Jesse,
said, "I need a new king who isn't so messy!"
So dad stood his 7 boys in one straight line,
and Samuel looked for one who would do the job fine.
But God said, "No!" So, Samuel asked for another,
"Isn't there another boy these guys call 'brother'"?
Jesse said, "Yeah, but he's the runt of the litter,
but when Samuel saw David, he knew no one could be fitter.
Well, David showed his faith when he faced a giant,
a giant named "Goliath" who was super defiant.
So with a stone from a sling, David hit him in the head,
and when the monster stopped rockin' he fell down dead!
Now David didn't just make giants meet their end,
he also became Jonathan's very best friend.
Twice the hit-man Saul's royal life he did spare,
an act of mercy that is very rare.
He also moved the Ark to Jerusalem city,
where the Temple would also one day be sitting.
Besides all this, he won every fight,
beatin' Philistines, Arameans and tough Ammonites.
So with all his success you wonder, "What could go wrong?"
Well, when spring rolled around it wouldn't take too long.

YOUR MISSION
What did God promise David about his throne?

_____

_____

_____

_____

_____

_____

_____

_____

_____

_____

_____

CLUES:
Read 2 Samuel 7:16

BIBLE RIDDLE #28

In the Spring while David was relaxin' at night.
Saw Bathsheba on her roof and he didn't do right.
To hide his sin he only made matters worse,
put her husband at the front for war so he'd die first.
Then had a family conflict with his son Absalom,
who wanted to steal his father's vast kingdom.
But when his hair got caught in a large oak tree,
it pretty much ended the conspiracy.
He also put all the soldiers names down,
a faithless act on which God did frown.
So bought a threshing floor to use as an altar,
and when he did that he no more did falter.
Now when his days as king were almost done,
he handed the baton to his son, Solomon.
So the promise began to the nation Israel,
that "he'd have a descendant on the throne" which wouldn't
fail.

YOUR MISSION

What did God command David's descendants to do
in order to keep a descendant of David on the throne?

_____

_____

_____

_____

_____

_____

_____

_____

_____

_____

CLUES:
Read 1 Kings 2:4

KING SOLOMON & OTHER KINGS

75

BIBLE RIDDLE #29

In a dream King Solomon asked to be wise,
and he turned out smarter than all the other guys.
And 'cause he didn't ask for great power or health,
God gave him all that along with great wealth.
So it happened as Solomon heard in his dream,
his wisdom and wealth and honor were *supreme*.
When the Queen of Sheba saw his wisdom and gold,
she declared, "Indeed half of is wasn't even told!"
He also built a Temple to worship the Lord,
a place where the praises of the people were poured.
But then he got careless with his 700 wives,
and that's not counting his 300 *concubines*.
The problem with these women was *idolatry*,
which broke their word to follow God's worship
decree. God said, "Since you disobeyed me, King
Solomon, Israel will be split in two and no longer one."
It happened fast with his son Rehoboam,
who would meet his match for the throne in Jeroboam.

YOUR MISSION

1. When Solomon asked for wisdom, what did God give him?
2. How did all of Solomon's wives affect his heart?

CLUES:

1. Read 1 Kings 3:11-13
2. Read 1 Kings 11:4

BIBLE RIDDLE #30

Since Solomon imported all his wives *idols*,
it ended up changing the nation's titles.
In the North there would be ten Jewish tribes,
and in the South only two on Rehoboam's side.
The Northern tribes were named, "Israel" with Jeroboam king,
and the South called "Judah" whom on Rehoboam did lean.
All because the true God Solomon did *betray*,
which led all the hearts of the people *astray*.
Then the story for Israel just kept getting worse,
when Jeroboam worshiped two golden calves first.
And Rehoboam did not do much better as king,
when he told the people "Obey me or you'll feel my scorpion sting!"
Yes, the rest of their history was really sad,
'cause a lot of the chosen people's kings were so bad.

YOUR MISSION
What became a sin for Israel?

_____
_____
_____
_____
_____
_____
_____
_____
_____
_____
_____

CLUES:
Read 1 Kings 12:28-30

BIBLE RIDDLE #31

Most of the North and South's kings were bad
highlighted by a little weasel named Ahab.
One big mistake was marrying his wife Jezebel,
who specialized in worshiping the god called Baal.
But there was good king Asa who fired his own grandma
for making an image of the goddess Asherah.
And Hezekiah who by Sennacherib was threatened,
took his fear to God, the one he *petitioned*.
Then the Assyrian Army died at the Word of the Lord,
and proud Sennacherib died by his own son's sword.
Still there was evil Manasseh who reigned really long --
55 years as a king doing wrong.
Like sacrificing children in a hot, hot fire
an act that really raised God's holy *ire*.
Practiced witchcraft, horoscopes and *divination*,
which to God were a gross *abomination*.
And since they despised God's word and messengers,
God had to send Babylonian avengers.
When they were done they'd ruined the holy city,
which no longer looked at all very pretty.
They also took the Jews far off to Babylon,
where for 70 years from home they were gone!

YOUR MISSION
Why did Jerusalem fall?

_____

_____

_____

_____

_____

_____

_____

_____

_____

_____

CLUES:
Read 2 Chronicles 36:15-19 (hint: key verse 16)

BIBLE RIDDLE #32

After Babylon came to Judah to invade,
they marched the best of Judah thru the desert in a parade.
They also left Jerusalem in a heap of rubble,
a city that had never seen so much trouble.
Like *looting* bronze and pots and shovels and dishes,
which went against Jerusalem's citizen's wishes.
Young men and women were by sharp swords *slayed*,
with no proper graves in which to be laid.
Even kids who hungered for a piece of bread,
were treated like they were already dead.
People's eyes failed from wailing and weeping,
from hundreds of years from their sins now reaping.
Now Jerusalem looked like an old ghost town,
since they marched so many people off this holy ground.
Then when they arrived in Babylonian land,
God gave his people a surprising command.
"Build houses, have children, eat your garden's good food,
and then your life will be really good!"

YOUR MISSION

What were the Jewish exiled supposed to seek for
the new city they were living in?

CLUES:

Read Jeremiah 29:7

BIBLE RIDDLE #33

There came along a Persian King named Cyrus,
whose return for the Jews to Jerusalem was *desirous.*
He said, "I want you to rebuild God's ruined house,"
something that would once again worship arouse.
And though like the first it's not in gold *adorned*
the second will be better with the glory of the Lord!
Then Nehemiah who tasted wine for a king,
said, "I'd like to get in on this rebuilding thing."
"But instead of *erecting* a downtown mall,
I'd like to rebuild the city's ruined wall."
Now when the wall in only 52 days was completed,
their enemies knew these Jews would not be defeated.
So the Jews in Babylon started to come back,
where no worship or word or safety they'd lack.
But still there remained one big unknown part,
who would conquer Judah's *wayward* heart?

YOUR MISSION

1. Who was God going to send to God's people?
2. What was this person going to do?

_____
_____
_____
_____
_____
_____
_____
_____
_____
_____
_____
_____

CLUES:

Read Malachi 4:5-6

JESUS

BIBLE RIDDLE #34

After years had passed there came a bundle of joy,
the first child born to a virgin, a sweet boy.
It wasn't easy when his stepdad almost left,
but then the angel said to Joseph, "He's God's gift!"
So, he and Mary walked to Bethlehem as strangers,
where Jesus was born at night in a cow's manger.
Soon shepherds who were watching their flocks at night,
saw an angel army in the sky that gave 'em a fright!
They said, "Don't be scared because as promised by Isaiah,
a child's been born in Bethlehem who's the Messiah!"
So, shepherds ran to the manger to check it out,
and when they saw the baby Jesus, they gave a great shout!
Now that he was here God's saving plan could start,
where Jesus would heal the people's sinful hearts.

YOUR MISSION
What does Jesus' name mean?

_____
_____
_____
_____
_____
_____
_____
_____
_____
_____
_____

CLUES:
Read Matthew 1:21

BIBLE RIDDLE #35

John the Baptist started his holy career,
eating honey, grasshoppers, and wearin' camel's hair.
His job was to prepare the Savior's grand entrance,
by preaching to the people a baptism of *repentance.*
Well, it happened at the Jordan where he saw the God-man,
John said, "Look, everyone, it's Jesus, God's Lamb!"
Then Jesus began to form his ministry troop,
a band of 12 disciples who'd be his training group.
For three years Jesus started doing all kinds of things,
the kind of things performed by the King of all kings.
Like curing blindness, opening deaf ears, raising the dead,
he also helped 10 *lepers* their diseased skin shed.
There were paralyzed men whom Jesus healed so they could walk,
and others kept from speaking who now could talk.
He also taught the wonders of the Kingdom of God,
and told everybody this should be their main job.
As you might expect the people loved him a lot,
after all he did to heal them and the freedom he brought!

YOUR MISSION
1. Who did Jesus say he was?
2. How do we come to the Father?

_____
_____
_____
_____
_____
_____
_____
_____
_____
_____
_____
_____

CLUES:
Read John 14:6

BIBLE RIDDLE #36

THE CROSS

At the urging of church leaders, the crowd's favor turned sour,
and Jesus' last week would be his darkest hour.
With jealousy and hate they would nail him to a cross,
and when they did that, it seemed all hope was lost.
At noon the sun went black and looked like it had failed,
when on the tree the body of the Christ was nailed.
But after three hours of doom and gloom,
some things began to happen hinting, "I spoke too soon!"
The earth did shake, some dead were raised, and Temple curtain torn,
which showed us Jesus' death just wasn't the norm.
What all the people then had no way to know,
was that His death meant victory over our *foe*!
You see, on that rugged cross Jesus bore our sin,
so that his righteousness could come to all men.
And though on that tree he looked graveyard dead,
instead it was Satan who wound up with a crushed head!

YOUR MISSION
1. Who became sin for us?
2. How did Jesus disarm and triumph over the powers and authorities?

CLUES:
1. Read 2 Corinthians 5:20-21
2. Read Colossians 2:15

BIBLE RIDDLE #37

THE RESURRECTION

So they took his body down,
and placed it in the cold ground.
Sealed the tomb where he was laid,
and thought for sure that's where he'd stay.
But God had a surprise,
when on the third day's sunrise,
God's power raised him from the dead
just like, before, Jesus said.
So now death has lost its bite,
for all those Jesus makes right.
And for all those who believe,
eternal life they'll receive!
Now can you think of something better,
than to live with God forever?
So why not receive his gift
and from God stop going *adrift*?

YOUR MISSION

1. What are some things we can receive from Jesus' resurrection?

_____
_____
_____
_____
_____
_____
_____
_____
_____
_____
_____
_____

CLUES:

Read 1 Peter 1:3-4

FOR RECEIVING GOD'S GIFT OF ETERNAL LIFE DO THIS:

Believe Jesus died on the cross for you and was raised to life - 1 Corinthians 15:2-4

Accept God's free forgiveness for your sins - Romans 3:22

Switch to God's plan for your life - Mark 8:34-38

Express your desire for Jesus to be the leader of your life - Romans 10:9

BEGINNINGS OF THE CHURCH

BIBLE RIDDLE #38

After Jesus rose from the dead there were some "loose ends,"
so he gathered on a mountain with his very best friends.
He said, "a gifts a-comin' to the world so in Jerusalem sit tight,
until the Holy Spirit comes in power and might."
After some days the Spirit came in fire and wind,
and after Peter preached, 3,000 turned from their sin!
When all those people in baptism were fully *immersed*,
they became the church, brand spankin' new and the first.
Soon together they were learning and praising the Lord…
talking, eating, praying, laughing and giving to the poor.
And tho' they saw great wonders and had gladness *galore*,
God saw a dying world and said, "There' so much more!"
so when some violent people started beating them down,
God used the attacks to move the church out of town.
And so the church did not do what you would think,
it started growing like a weed and did not shrink.
For God had planned for all the world the Savior to know,
and that could only happen if his people would go!

YOUR MISSION

1. Where did Jesus tell his disciples that they would be his witnesses?
2. Who would help them accomplish this mission?

CLUES:

Read Acts 1:8

BIBLE RIDDLE #39

One day the Church's enemy named Paul,
was riding to Damascus when he got God's call.
Jesus said, "Why do you keep beatin' up on my bride,*
don't you know that it's for her I died?"
"Now, go take my message to 'Gentiles' (non-Jews),
it's time for everybody to hear the good news."
So, Paul sailed all over the Mediterranean,
tellin' people how they could be born again.
From Ephesus to Rome and Philippi,
to Galatia and Corinth and troubled Colossae.
Even when he got attacked and whipped,
no amount of beating could keep his mouth zipped.
He preached, "Faith in Jesus makes you right with God,"
a message Paul spread everywhere and abroad.
Also, "Let the Holy Spirit give you a lift,
then watch what God will give to you for a gift."
"And you were made to be like Jesus, God's Son,
so rise to the challenge and with sin be done."
This good news started going to the ends of the earth,
defeating sin's curse with the Spirit's new birth!

YOUR MISSION

1. Who did Paul say we were predestined to be like, or conformed to?
2. What were we chosen to be like before the world was created?

CLUES:

1. Read Romans 8:29
2. Read Ephesians 1:4

NOTE: Although Jesus did not have a wife, you will hear people refer to Jesus' bride. The Bible sometimes refers to the Church as his bride to show the importance of how much he loves the church, treasures it, and would give himself up for her to make her clean and beautiful. In this riddle, I am saying that Jesus is asking does he keep killing and abusing his Church, his followers. (Revelations 19:7; Ephesians 5:25-27)

HEAVEN

BIBLE RIDDLE #40

God's great plan is bigger than just this world,
He has loads of joy for grown-ups and boys and girls.
In place of Eden there will be another Garden,
a Garden made to play in for all those *pardoned*.
There'll also be a house made just for friends and you,
a house with lots of things for all your friends to do.
It won't be sad 'cause there'll be no crying or tears,
and that's the way it'll be for endless days and years.
Then your new body'll be packed with power and glory,
something you'll live in to write a brand new story.
There'll be a city made with golden streets and gates of pearl,
and beautiful colors like sapphire, ruby, and *beryl*.
And beyond the streets and pearly gates and spacious homes,
will be a park-like setting where you're free to roam.
With sparkling clear water and a twelve-fruit tree,
and healing for everyone coming from the leaves.
So don't be left outside all of Heaven's wonder,
'cause that would be your life's biggest *blunder*!
Instead wash your clothes real clean and white and pretty,
just trust Christ to forgive you, then enter the city.
And when that time comes to get your Heavenly start,
you'll say, "This is by far the very best part!"

YOUR MISSION

1. What happens to the people whose names aren't written in the "book of life"?
2. What happens to the person who opens the door of their heart to Jesus?

CLUES:

1. Read Revelation 20:15
2. Read Revelation 3:20

ACTION: Ask Jesus to forgive your sin and come into your life

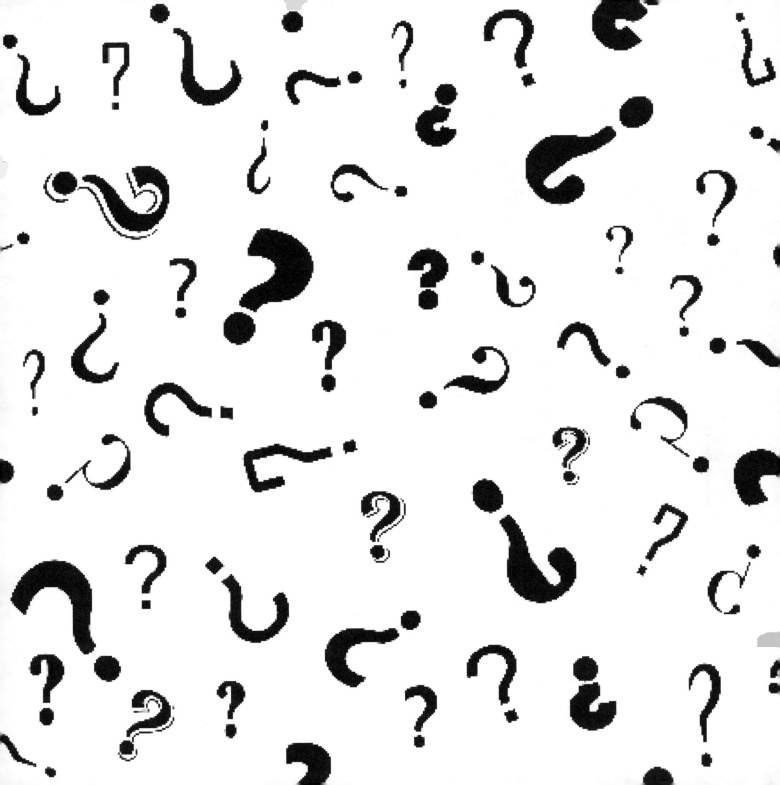

BIBLE RIDDLES ANSWER KEY

1. With His words.
2. People.
3. To create a family and take care of the animals.
4. He thought it was very good.
5. He rested.
6. a. Tree of the knowledge of good and evil.
 b. He would die.
7. a. They saw that they were naked.
 b. Made clothes out of fig leaves.
 c. They hid from God.
8. a. He was cursed to crawl on his belly.
 b. She would experience great pain in childbearing and be ruled by her husband.
 c. The ground would be cursed, making it hard to work for food, and he would die.
9. Garments of skin.
10. They called on the name of the Lord, which is prayer.
11. a. Methuselah; 969 years.
 b. Enoch; He walked with God.
12. a. Noah.
 b. A boat.
 c. Noah, his family and animals.
 d. To keep the animals alive.
13. Abram (whose name was later changed to "Abraham", Genesis 17:5).

14. a. 20 shekels of silver.
 b. Egypt.
 c. Potiphar.
15. a. Potiphar.
 b. Potiphar's wife.
 c. He could interpret Pharaoh's dreams.
16. a. Judah.
 b. Save lives.
17. a. He threw them into the Nile river.
 b. In a basket hidden in the reeds.
 c. Moses.
18. a. Because he was standing on Holy ground.
 b. That God would be with him.
 c. I Am.
19. a. The death of Egypt's firstborn son.
 b. Passover.
20. They feared the Lord and put their trust in him and in Moses.
21. a. Marah.
 b. Meat and bread.
22. a. You shall have no other gods before me.
 b. Honor your father and your mother.
 c. You shall not steal.
23. a. The Lord God.
 b. The Jordan river
 c. It stopped flowing.

24. The Lord.

25. They did whatever they wanted.

26. He plundered all the goods and did evil in the eyes of God.

27. It would endure forever.

28. To watch how they live and to walk faithfully with God with all their heart and soul.

29. a. Wisdom, wealth and honor.

 b. They turned his heart to follow other gods.

30. They worshiped golden calves, which were false gods.

31. They mocked God's messengers, despised his words and scoffed at his prophets.

32. The peace and prosperity of the city.

33. a. Elijah.

 b. Turn the hearts or the fathers to the children and the hearts of the children to their fathers.

34. God saves.

35. a. The way and the truth and the life.

 b. Through Jesus.

36. a. Jesus Christ.

 b. By the cross.

37. A living hope and an inheritance that will never perish, spoil or fade.

38. a. In Jerusalem, all Judea and Samaria and, to the ends of the earth.

 b. The Holy Spirit.

39. a. His Son, Jesus.

 b. To be holy and blameless in his sight.

40. a. They will be thrown in to the lake of fire.

b. He will live in our hearts.

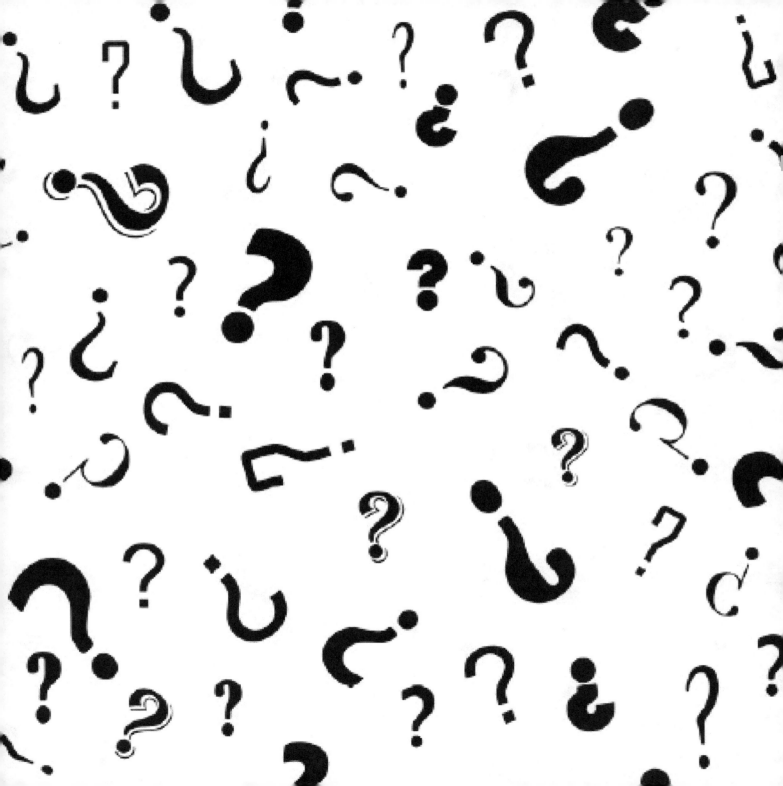

GLOSSARY

Abomination: something that is detestable, hated, or abhorred.

Adrift: not anchored, as a boat; drifting.

Adorned: to add beauty to; decorate.

Alfalfa: a plant with purple flowers that is grown as food for cattle and horses. Alfalfa is a member of the legume family of plants.

Astray: off the right or known path or course.

Baals: a false god or idol, esp. according to the Hebrews.

Baton: a staff denoting position or authority.

Beryl: a crystalline mineral, aluminum beryllium silicate, from which beryllium and certain gemstones such as emeralds are derived.

Betray: to not be loyal or faithful to.

Blunder: to make a silly, careless, or stupid mistake.

Concubine: a woman who cohabits with a man but is not married to him; mistress.

Conspiracy: a secret agreement among two or more people to do something wrong or illegal; plot.

Crave: to need or desire very much.

Credentials: something that entitles one to confidence, credit, privilege, or authority.

Curse: to make a statement that wishes harm on someone.

Decree: an official order or decision by a ruler or government.

Defiant: showing no respect for authority; refusing to obey.

Deliverer: to send or bring to a particular person or place.

Deluge: a huge amount.

Descendant: one who comes from a given ancestor or ancestors.

Desirous: having desire; desiring.

Devastation: the act or an instance of destroying or ruining, or the destruction or ruin thus caused. Overwhelmed

Divination: the act of prophecy or revelation by interpreting omens or by supernatural means.

Egad: (old fashioned) a mild oath used to express surprise or enthusiasm.

Enticed: to lure or tempt, as by calling attention to the possible benefits of an action.

Erecting: upright in posture or position.

Falter: to move, speak, or act in a way that is not sure or not steady; stumble.

Foe: one who wishes ill on another; personal enemy.

Furrowed: any narrow groove in a surface.

Galore: in great numbers; abundantly.

Grieving: to feel great sadness; mourn.

Highness: a title of honor used when speaking to or about a royal person

Idolatry: the worship of idols.

Idols: a statue or image of a god that is used as an object of worship.

Immersed: to almost cover or cover completely with liquid.

Influential: having power or influence.

Ire: anger or wrath.

Lair: a wild animal's shelter; den.

Lepers: a person afflicted with leprosy.

Looting: goods taken by stealing or other dishonest means.

Obediently: likely or willing to obey rules or orders.

Oppressing: to treat in a way that is cruel or not fair.

Pardoned: an official act that frees a person from punishment for a crime.

Petitioned: a formal, written request by many people that is made to a person in authority.

Plagues: a deadly disease, sudden invasion of harmful insects, or any terrible thing that harms many people.

Precision: the state of being accurate or exact.

Rebellion: the act of disobeying rules or fighting against authority.

Reign: rule by a king or queen.

Repentance: the feeling of sorrow or deep regret for something done in the past.

Reptilian: low, contemptible, or treacherous.

Slayed: to kill deliberately and violently.

Steer: to make something move in a certain direction.

Sterling: excellent or very fine.

Supreme: having the highest rank, position, or authority.

Taint: to tarnish, as with moral wrongness.

Teeter: to cause to wobble or be unsteady.

Temptation: the act or an instance of tempting, or the condition of being tempted.

Threshing: to separate the grain from the chaff of (a cereal such as wheat)

Tussle: to fight or struggle roughly or energetically; scuffle.

Uniting: to bring together for a common purpose.

Vast: very large in size or area.

Wayward: difficult to control; willfully disobedient.

Widow: a woman whose husband has died.

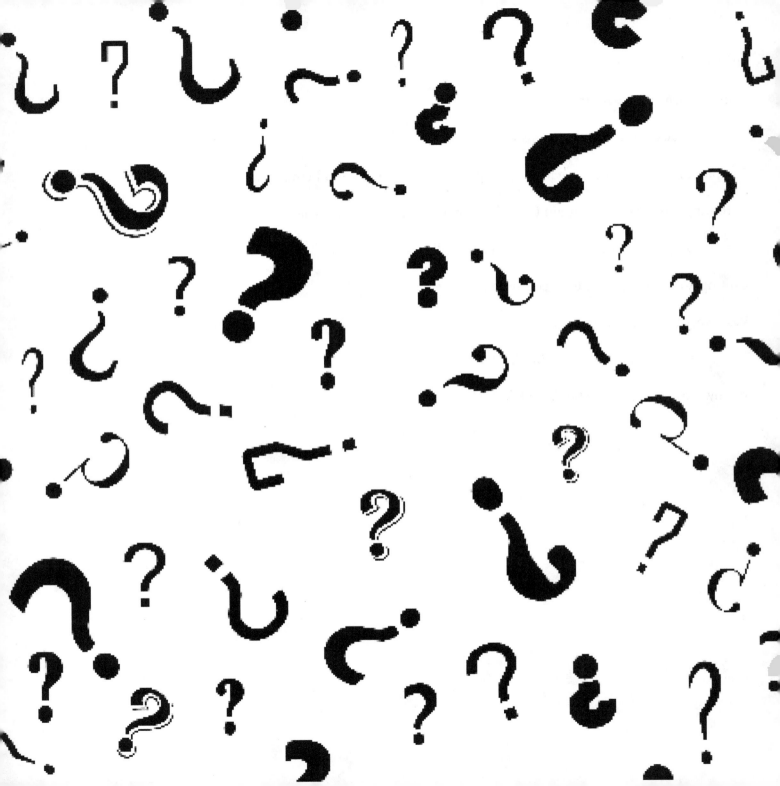

**FOR MORE BOOKS LIKE THIS
VISIT WWW.HONEYDROPKIDS.COM**

CPSIA information can be obtained
at www.ICGtesting.com
Printed in the USA
BVHW011956210222
629709BV00012B/495

9 781088 007877